CONTENTS

4B

KB101616

UNIT 1
What Do You Do on Weekends?

Mini Talk Look and listen. ▶ 🎧03

What do you do on weekends?

I take a dance class.

I ride my bike.

What about you?

CHECK 🎧04

1   What does the girl do on weekends?   a ☐ b ☐
2   Does the boy ride his bike on weekends?   a ☐ b ☐

Practice

A Listen and write the letter. 🎧05 **B** Listen and repeat. 🎧06

What do you do on weekends? | I watch sports.

1. watch sports ☐
2. read books ☐
3. bake bread ☐
4. go to the farm ☐
5. have soccer practice ☐
6. ride my bike ☐
7. clean my room ☐
8. wash my dog ☐

Listen & Talk

A Listen and match. 🎧07

1
 •　　　•　on Tuesdays　•　　　•　

2
 •　　　•　on Saturdays　•　　　•　

3
 •　　　•　on weekends　•　　　•　

4
 •　　　•　on Fridays　•　　　•　

5
 •　　　•　on Sundays　•　　　•　

YOUR TURN B Check and say.

What do you do on weekends?

I _____.

read books ☐

ride my bike ☐

clean my room ☐

Write & Talk

A Write, listen, and read. 08

Sam: What do you do on _____?

Amy: I usually go to the _____.

Sam: What do you do there?

Amy: I _____ my uncle.

Sam: Sounds good.

Amy: What _____ you, Sam?

Sam: I have _____ on Saturdays.

soccer practice	help	farm	Saturdays	about

B Look and write. Then say.

 1 on weekends

 2 on Thursdays

 3 on Saturdays

1 I _____ on weekends.

2 He _____ on Thursdays.

3 She _____ on Saturdays.

goes to the park

takes a robot class

watch sports

Reading

Jane goes to the library on Saturdays.

She reads many books there.

She watches movies, too.

She is busy on Saturdays.

Tom cleans his room on weekends.

And he washes his dog.

He bakes bread with Mom, too.

He is busy on weekends.

B Circle or write.

1 Jane goes to the library (on Saturdays / on Sundays).

2 She (watches sports / watches movies) in the library.

3 Tom cleans his room _____ .

Build Up

Ⓐ Listen and repeat. 🎧10

-s / -es / -ies

play – plays	wash – washes	study – studies
clean – cleans	watch – watches	fly – flies
bake – bakes	go – goes	

Ⓑ Change and write.

1

bake cookies

He _____ on Wednesdays.

2

go swimming

She _____ on Saturdays.

3

wash her dog

My sister _____ on Thursdays.

4

fly a kite

Betty _____ on Sundays.

5

study English

Steve _____ on Mondays.

Check-Up

A Listen and number. 🎧11

B Listen and choose. 🎧12

1  ⓐ ⓑ

2  ⓐ ⓑ

3  ⓐ ⓑ

4  ⓐ ⓑ

C Listen and circle. 🎧13

1 Susan

She (takes a dance class / bakes bread) on Fridays.

2 Fred

He (cleans his room / watches sports) on weekends.

8

D Look and write.

1

A: What do you do _____ weekends?

B: I _____.

2

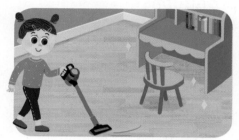

A: What _____ she do on Tuesdays?

B: She _____.

3

A: I _____ my bike on Sundays.

What about you?

B: I _____.

E Write and say.

1

A: What do you do on Saturdays?

B: _____

2

A: What do you do on weekends?

B: _____

How Many Balloons Do You Have?

Mini Talk Look and listen.

Do you have balloons?

Yes, I do.

How many balloons do you have?

I have five balloons.

Happy birthday, Max!

CHECK 17

1 What does the girl have?   a ☐   b ☐

2 How many balloons does she have?   a ☐   b ☐

Practice

(A) Listen and write the letter. 🎧18

(B) Listen and repeat. 🎧19

How many cupcakes do you have?

I have six cupcakes.

1. cupcakes ☐

2. apple pies ☐

3. donuts ☐

4. plates ☐

5. forks ☐

6. spoons ☐

7. candles ☐

8. party hats ☐

Listen & Talk

A Listen and match. 🎧 20

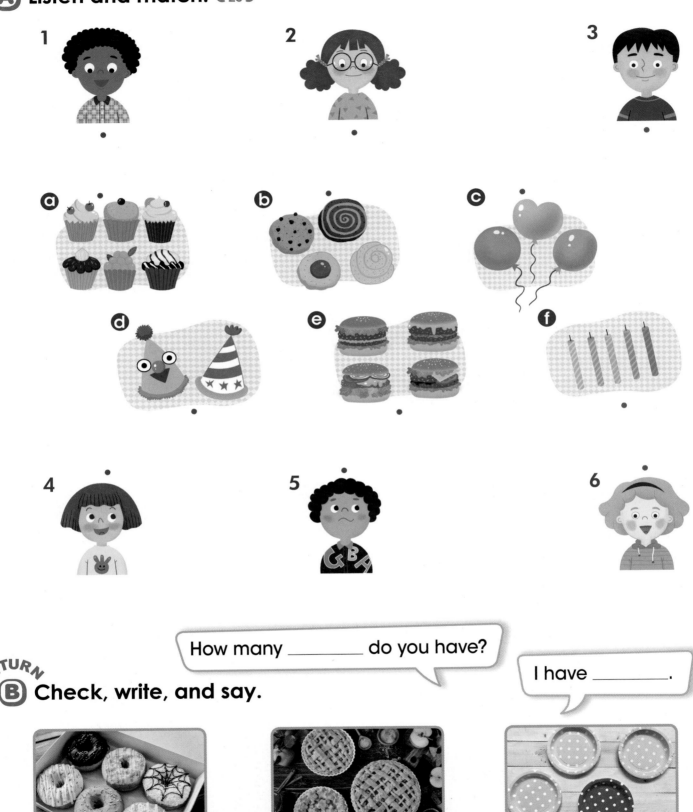

1

2

3

a

b

c

d

e

f

4

5

6

YOUR TURN

B Check, write, and say.

How many _____ do you have?

I have _____.

_____ donuts

_____ apple pies

_____ plates

12

Write & Talk

Ⓐ Write, listen, and read. 🎧 21

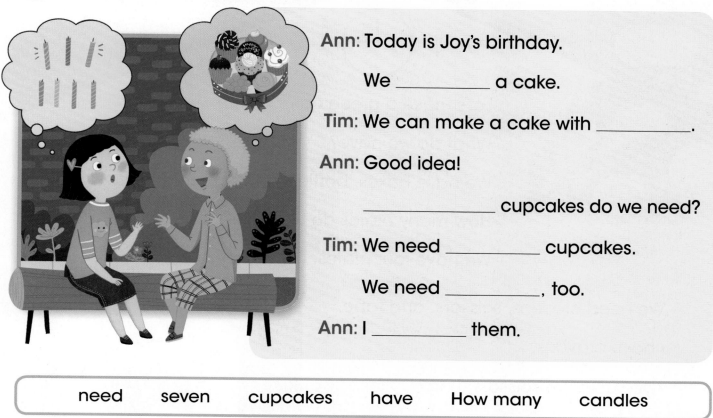

Ann: Today is Joy's birthday.

We _____ a cake.

Tim: We can make a cake with _____.

Ann: Good idea!

_____ cupcakes do we need?

Tim: We need _____ cupcakes.

We need _____, too.

Ann: I _____ them.

| need | seven | cupcakes | have | How many | candles |

Ⓑ Look and write. Then ask and answer.

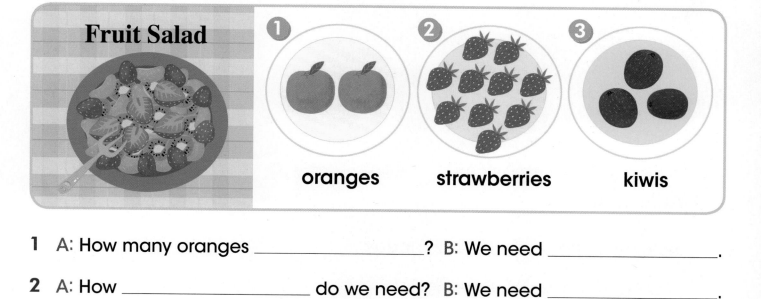

Fruit Salad

1 oranges   2 strawberries   3 kiwis

1 A: How many oranges _____? B: We need _____.

2 A: How _____ do we need? B: We need _____.

3 A: _____ do we need?   B: _____

Reading

Let's make a green car.

What do we have?

We have boxes, bottles, and paper plates.

How many plates do we have?

We have four plates.

We need crayons, scissors, and tape.

I have crayons.

"Do you have scissors, Tina?"

"Yes, I do. I have tape, too."

"That's good."

Wow! We have a nice car now.

Ⓑ **Write or circle.**

1 They're making _____ today.

2 They have six paper plates.   (T / F)

3 They have scissors. But they don't have tape.   (T / F)

14

Build Up

A Listen and repeat. 🎧 23

 How many cupcakes do you have?   I have five cupcakes.

 How many apples do you need?   I need three apples.

 How many cookies do you want?   I want two cookies.

B Look and write.

1

A: _____ do you have?

B: I have seven crayons.

2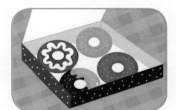

A: _____ do you want?

B: I want four donuts.

3

A: _____ do you need?

B: I need three forks.

4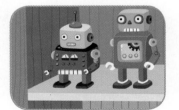

A: _____ do you have?

B: I have two robots.

5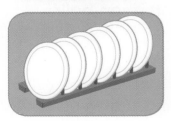

A: _____ do we need?

B: We need six plates.

Check-Up

Ⓐ Listen and number. 🎧24

▢ ▢ ▢ ▢

Ⓑ Listen and choose. 🎧25

1  ⓐ ⓑ

2  ⓐ ⓑ

3  ⓐ ⓑ

4  ⓐ ⓑ

Ⓒ Listen and choose. 🎧26

1 Cathy has _____.

　ⓐ three candles　　　ⓑ three balloons　　　ⓒ thirteen balls

2 They need _____.

　ⓐ eleven plates　　　ⓑ eleven forks　　　ⓒ twelve plates

D Look, write, and match.

1 _____ do you want? •   • I have eight balloons.

2 _____ do you need? •   • I need ten candles.

3 _____ do you have? •   • I want four cupcakes.

E Write and say.

1

A: _____

B: I have eight donuts.

2

A: How many spoons do you need?

B: _____

Review ①

Ⓐ Look and write.

How many forks do you have?	What do you do on Thursdays?
Do you have forks?	

Taday is Thursday.

_____

I have a baking class.

Sounds great.

I have some cake.

_____

Yes, I do.

The Next Day

_____

I have two forks.

B Read and write the number.

1 A: What do they do on Fridays?

   B: They read books.

2 A: What does he do on Sundays?

   B: He has piano practice.

3 A: What do you do on weekends?

   B: I ride my bike.

C Write and match.

1
A: _____ do you have?

B: I _____ six cupcakes.

a

2
A: _____ do you want?

B: I _____ two donuts.

b

3
A: _____ do we need?

B: We _____ five plates.

c

May I Come In?

Mini Talk Look and listen. ▶ 🎧29

May I come in?

No Dogs

Yes, you may. Come in, please.

Sorry. You can't bring your dog. You can use that.

Oh, I see.

P

CHECK 🎧30

Listen and check.

1 T ☐ F ☐   2 T ☐ F ☐

Practice

A Listen and write the letter. 🎧31

B Listen and repeat. 🎧32

May I drink some juice?	Yes, you may. / No, you may not.

drink some juice

use my phone

use the computer

borrow your pen

LIBRARY CARD

come in

go to the restroom

bring my dog

sit here

Listen & Talk

A Listen, number, and circle. 🎧 33

May I _____?

Yes, you may. / No, you may not.

YOUR TURN
B Check and say.

bring my dog

go to the restroom

use my phone

22

Write & Talk

A Write, listen, and read. 🎧 34

Tim: May I _____ some juice here?

Driver: No, you _____.

Tim: _____ I eat some sandwiches?

Driver: No, you may not.

You can't _____ on the bus.

Tim: _____, I see.

May	drink	may not	eat	Okay

B Look and write. Then ask and answer.

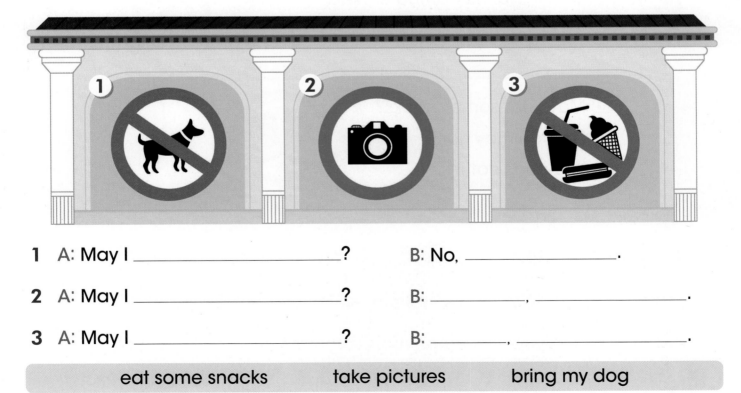

1 A: May I _____?   B: No, _____.

2 A: May I _____?   B: _____, _____.

3 A: May I _____?   B: _____, _____.

eat some snacks   take pictures   bring my dog

Reading

Ⓐ Listen and read. 🎧35

Fun Children's Library Q&A

Q: May I borrow books?

A: Yes, you may.
Please make a library card.

LIBRARY CARD
1234567
0000

Q: May I bring my hamster?

A: No, you may not bring animals in the library.

Q: May I use my phone?

A: No, you may not.
You can use it outside.

Q: May I use the computer here?

A: Yes, you may. We have ten computers.

Q: May I eat some snacks?

A: No, you may not.
You can't eat inside.

Ⓑ Read and circle.

1 You (may / may not) eat snacks in the library.

2 You (may / may not) bring animals in the library.

3 You (may / may not) use the computers in the library.

Build Up

A Listen and repeat. 🎧 36

May I ~? / Can I ~?

May I eat some food here?
Yes, you may. / No, you may not.

Can I sit here?
Yes, you can. / No, you can't.

B Write and circle.

1

A: _____ your ruler?

B: (Yes, you can. / No, you can't.)

2

A: _____ a picture?

B: (Yes, you may. / No, you may not.)

3

A: _____ the cake?

B: (Yes, you can. / No, you can't.)

4

A: _____ this car?

B: (Yes, you may. / No, you may not.)

5

A: _____ to the restroom?

B: (Yes, you may. / No, you may not.)

---

take

borrow

touch

eat

go

Check-Up

A Listen and check. 🎧37

1

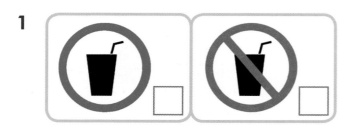

2

3

4

B Listen, number, and circle. 🎧38

C Listen and circle. 🎧39

1 The boy needs (scissors / an eraser).

2 The girl (can / can't) eat food in the museum.

D Look and write.

1

A: May I _____?

B: Yes, you _____.

2

A: May I _____?

B: No, you _____.

3

A: May I _____?

B: Sure.

E Write and say.

1

A: _____

B: Yes, you may.

2

A: _____

B: No, you may not.

UNIT 4 My Favorite Subject Is Music

Mini Talk Look and listen. ▶ 🎧42

MUSIC ROOM

What's your favorite subject?

My favorite subject is music.

Do you like to sing songs?

No, I don't. I like to play the drums.

🎧 CHECK 43

Listen and check.

1 T ☐ F ☐   2 T ☐ F ☐

Practice

Ⓐ Listen and write the letter. 🎧44 **Ⓑ Listen and repeat.** 🎧45

What's your favorite subject?

My favorite subject is math.

I like to study math.

Listen & Talk

A Listen and match. 🎧 46

1 •

 •

•  **a**

2 •

 •

•  **b**

3 •

 •

•  **c**

4 •

 •

•  **d**

5 •

 •

•  **e**

YOUR TURN
B Check and say.

My favorite subject is _____.

I like to _____.

speak English

sing songs

read maps

Write & Talk

A Write, listen, and read. 47

Amy: Do you _____ science books?

Tom: Yes, _____ .

Amy: What's your _____ subject?

Tom: My favorite subject is _____ .

I like to _____ the stars.

They're beautiful.

| favorite | I do | science | like | watch |

B Match and write. Then ask and answer.

1 sport

lion

2 fruit

mango

3 animal

baseball

1 A: What's your favorite sport?

B: My favorite _____ is _____ .

2 A: What's your favorite _____ ?

B: My _____ is the _____ .

3 A: What's your _____ ?

B: My _____ is the _____ .

Reading

A Listen and read. 🎧 48

My name is Susan.

My favorite subject is art.

I like to draw animals.

I draw many cats and dogs.

Do you like my pictures?

Chris likes to make animal cookies.

He bakes cookies on Saturdays.

The animal cookies are cute.

I like them!

B Circle or choose.

1   Susan's favorite subject is (art / music).

2   She likes to (play with animals / draw animals).

3   What does Chris do on Saturdays?

ⓐ He watches movies.   ⓑ He bakes cookies.   ⓒ He takes a cooking class.

Build Up

A Listen and repeat. 49

I like to read books.

She likes to sing songs.

like to, likes to

B Look and write.

read   drink   listen   play   watch

1

I like to _____ to music.

2

He _____ basketball.

3

I _____ English books.

4

Mark _____ movies.

5

Jane _____ milk.

Check-Up

A Listen and match. 🎧50

1

2

3

4

· · · ·

· · · ·

B Listen and number. 🎧51

 ☐

 ☐

 ☐

 ☐

C Listen and circle T or F. 🎧52

1 Jane likes to read maps.   (T / F)

2 Simon's favorite animal is the dog.   (T / F)

D Look and write.

1

A: _____ your favorite subject?

B: My _____ is math.

2

My favorite subject is _____.

I like to _____.

3

A: Do you like to _____?

B: Yes, I do. My favorite subject is _____.

E Write and say.

1

A: What's your favorite subject?

B: _____

   I like to sing songs.

2

A: What's your favorite subject?

B: _____

   I like to play sports.

A **Look and write.**

> May I bring my turtle? I like to listen to music. Yes, you may.
>
> May I bring my donuts? No, you may not.

B Match and write the number.

1 My favorite subject is art. • • I like to play sports.

2 My favorite subject is P.E. • • I like to read maps.

3 My favorite subject is social studies. • • I like to draw pictures.

C Look and write the letter.

Sure.

No, you may not.

Yes, you may.

No, you may not.

ⓐ May I use the computer?　ⓑ May I sit here?

ⓒ May I come in?　ⓓ May I borrow your pen?

We'll Make Cookies Tomorrow

Mini Talk Look and listen. ▶ 55

Hi, Bill. Do you have a violin lesson tomorrow?

No, I don't.

We'll make cookies tomorrow. Can you join us?

Sure. Sounds fun.

Practice

A Listen and write the letter. 🎧57   **B** Listen and repeat. 🎧58

I'll make cookies tomorrow. Can you join me?

Sure.

make cookies ☐

pick apples ☐

plant trees ☐

catch fish ☐

meet Nick ☐

have a picnic ☐

play games ☐

go to the water park ☐

Listen & Talk

A Listen and match. 🎧 59

1

2

3

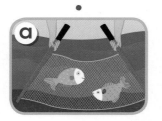
a

b

c

d

e

4

5

YOUR TURN
B Check and say.

I'll _____ tomorrow.

go to the water park ☐

meet friends ☐

make cookies ☐

Write & Talk

Ⓐ Write, listen, and read. 🎧60

Ben: I'll go to the water park _____.

Can you _____ me?

Jim: Sorry, _____. I'll study English.

Ben: Really? Jane _____ join me.

We'll _____ in the water. We'll eat snacks.

Jim: With Jane? Okay. I'll go with you.

| will | tomorrow | I can't | join | play |

Ⓑ Write and check. Then ask and answer.

1

A: I'll _____ tomorrow.

Can you join me?

B: ☐ Sure.   ☐ Sorry, I can't.

> catch fireflies
> pick tomatoes
> plant flowers

2

A: I'll _____ tomorrow.

Can you join me?

B: ☐ Sure.   ☐ Sorry, I can't.

3

A: We'll _____ tomorrow.

Can you join us?

B: ☐ Sure.   ☐ Sorry, I can't.

Reading

A Listen and read. 🎧 61

Tomorrow is Saturday.

My family will go to Uncle's farm.

Uncle has many orange trees.

We will pick oranges and make pies.

In the afternoon, we will go to the river.

We will catch big fish.

We will eat the fish for dinner.

It will be fun. I can't wait!

B Circle or choose.

1   The boy will go to (Uncle's shop / Uncle's farm) tomorrow.

2   He will (pick apples / make orange pies) there.

3   He will _____ in the afternoon.

    ⓐ pick oranges   **ⓑ** make pies   **ⓒ** catch fish

Build Up

A Listen and repeat. 🎧62

I'll ⋯→ I will
We'll ⋯→ We will
He'll ⋯→ He will
They'll ⋯→ They will

I will make cookies tomorrow.

He will go camping this weekend.

B Look and write.

have a picnic   bake bread   play baseball   meet friends   fly a drone

1

I will _____ this weekend.

2

He _____ tomorrow.

3

We _____ tomorrow.

4

He _____ next weekend.

5

My family _____ this Saturday.

Check-Up

A Listen and choose. 🎧 63

1  ⓐ ⓑ

2  ⓐ ⓑ

3  ⓐ ⓑ

4  ⓐ ⓑ

B Listen and number. 🎧 64

 ☐

 ☐

 ☐

 ☐

C Listen and choose. 🎧 65

1 Sue will _____ tomorrow.

  ⓐ go to the farm   ⓑ watch a movie   ⓒ watch sports

2 They will _____ this weekend.

  ⓐ have a party   ⓑ have a picnic   ⓒ go camping

D Look and write.

1

A: I'll _____ tomorrow.

Can you join me?

B: Sure.

2

A: I'll _____ this weekend.

Can you join me?

B: Sorry, I can't. I have a piano lesson.

3

A: We'll _____ tomorrow.

Can you _____ us?

B: Sure. Sounds fun.

E Write and say.

1

tomorrow

A: _____

Can you join me?

B: Sure.

2

this weekend

A: _____

Can you join us?

B: Sorry, I can't.

UNIT 6

What Will You Do This Summer?

Mini Talk Look and listen. ▶ 68

I'll go to the beach with my family.

What will you do this summer, Fred?

I'll take funny pictures.

It sounds fun.

● CHECK 69

1 What will Fred do this summer? a ☐ b ☐
2 What will he do there? a ☐ b ☐

Practice

A Listen and write the letter. 🎧70   **B** Listen and repeat. 🎧71

What will you do this summer?	I'll go on a trip.

1 go on a trip ☐

2 go to the beach ☐

3 visit my grandparents ☐

4 visit the art museum ☐

5 learn Chinese ☐

6 read many books ☐

7 take swimming lessons ☐

8 join a summer camp ☐

Listen & Talk

A Listen and number. 🎧 72

YOUR TURN

B Check and say.

What will you do this summer?

I'll _____.

visit the art museum

join a summer camp

go to the beach

48

Write & Talk

A Write, listen, and read. 🎧73

Brian: What will you do _____?

Eva: _____ go to the beach.

Brian: What _____ you do there?

Eva: I'll swim with my friend.

I'll _____ a boat, too.

Brian: Sounds great. _____ a good time.

Eva: You, too.

I'll	ride	will	this weekend	Have

B Look and write. Then ask and answer.

① this weekend

② this summer

③ this winter

1 A: What will you do this weekend?   B: I _____.

2 A: What will Junho do this summer?   B: He _____.

3 A: What will Kate do this winter?   B: _____.

learn English	go hiking	join a ski camp

Reading

(A) Listen and read. 🎧 74

Dear Tiara,

How are you?

I'm good.

What will you do this winter?

I will go on a trip to Sydney.

It will be summer there.

I will go to the beach.

I will go to the zoo and meet koalas.

I will join a summer Christmas party, too.

Your friend,
Alice

(B) Write or circle.

1 Alice will _____ this winter.

2 She will ski in Sydney.   (T / F)

3 She will go to the zoo.   (T / F)

Build Up

A Listen and repeat. 75

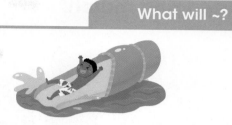

What will ~?

What will you do tomorrow?
I will visit the art museum.

What will he do this summer?
He will go to the water park.

B Look and write.

| meet | join | clean | read | go |

1

A: What _____ you _____ this winter?

B: I will _____ a winter camp.

2

A: What _____ you do tomorrow?

B: We _____ _____ Cindy.

3

A: What _____ he _____ this summer?

B: _____ many books.

4

A: What _____ she _____ this weekend?

B: _____ her room.

5

A: What _____ they _____ this Sunday?

B: _____ fishing.

Check-Up

A Listen and match. 76

1
2
3
4

a
b
c
d

B Listen and choose. 77

1  a b

2  a b

3  a b

4  a b

C Listen and circle. 78

1 Max will (learn Chinese / learn English) this summer.

2 Lily will (ride a bike / go on a trip) this winter.

D Look and write.

1

summer

A: What _____ you do this _____?

B: I'll _____ swimming lessons.

2

A: We'll _____ the art museum.

B: _____ a good time.

3

tomorrow

A: _____ will you do _____?

B: I'll _____ many books at home.

E Write and say.

1

A: What will you do this summer?

B: _____

2

A: What will you do this weekend?

B: _____

Ⓐ Look and write.

> What will you do there?
>
> What will you do this winter?
>
> I'll go to China.
>
> We'll play together.

Ⓑ Look and write.

1

A: What will you do this summer?

B: I'll _____.

2

A: What will you do this winter?

B: I _____.

3

A: My family _____ tomorrow.

B: Have a good time.

4

A: What will she do this weekend?

B: She _____.

5

A: We _____ this Sunday.

   Can you join us?

B: Sorry, I can't. I'm busy.

---

have a picnic   make cookies   plant trees

read many books   join a summer camp

What Did You Do Yesterday?

Mini Talk Look and listen. ▶ 🎧 81

What did you do yesterday?

I played computer games. What did you do?

I did my homework.

Homework?

● CHECK 🎧 82

1 What did the boy do yesterday?   a ☐   b ☐
2 What did the girl do yesterday?   a ☐   b ☐

Practice

A Listen and write the letter. 🎧 83   **B** Listen and repeat. 🎧 84

| What did you do yesterday? | I listened to music. |

1 listened to music ☐

2 cleaned my room ☐

3 visited my aunt ☐

4 stayed home ☐

5 helped my dad ☐

6 played badminton ☐

7 watched a movie ☐

Listen & Talk

A Listen and number. 🎧 85

YOUR TURN
B Check and say.

What did you do yesterday?

I _____.

played basketball

helped my dad

watched a movie

Write & Talk

A Write, listen, and read. 🎧86

Bill: What did you do _____?

Lily: I _____ home all day.

I _____ my dog. How about you?

Bill: I _____ my mom.

I _____ bread with her.

Lily: Sounds good.

| yesterday | washed | stayed | baked | helped |

What did he/she do yesterday?

B Look and write. Then ask and answer.

 1  2  3  4

1 He _____.

2 She _____.

3 He _____.

4 She _____.

listened to music

played baseball

cleaned her room

visited his uncle

Reading

Dan visited his grandfather yesterday.

He had a great time with his grandfather.

They played computer games.

They listened to rap music and danced, too.

Rap music is Dan's favorite music.

At night, they watched the stars together.

"The stars are beautiful."

It was a great day for Dan.

B Circle or choose.

1 Dan visited his grandfather (today / yesterday).

2 His grandfather (can / can't) play computer games.

3 He _____ with his grandfather at night.

   ⓐ played badminton   ⓑ cleaned the house   ⓒ watched the stars

Build Up

A Listen and repeat. 88

-ed

stay – stay**ed**   play – play**ed**   help – help**ed**   listen – listen**ed**
visit – visit**ed**   clean – clean**ed**   watch – watch**ed**   wash – wash**ed**

I listen to music every day.   I listened to music yesterday.

He plays badminton on Saturdays.   He played badminton yesterday.

B Change and write.

1 I _____ my friend yesterday.

2 We _____ our house yesterday.

3 Tina _____ home yesterday.

4 My uncle _____ his car yesterday.

5 They _____ a basketball game yesterday.

clean
watch
wash
visit
stay

Check-Up

A Listen and check. 🎧89

1

2

3

4

B Listen and choose. 🎧90

1 ⓐ ⓑ ⓒ

2 ⓐ ⓑ ⓒ

3 ⓐ ⓑ ⓒ

4 ⓐ ⓑ ⓒ

C Listen and circle. 🎧91

1 Nancy (cleaned her room / listened to music) yesterday.

2 Kevin (played computer games / did his homework) yesterday.

D Look and write.

1

A: What _____ you do yesterday?

B: I _____ the windows.

2

A: What _____ Kate _____ yesterday?

B: She _____ her mom.

3

A: What _____ he _____ yesterday?

B: He _____ a movie with friends.

E Write and say.

1

A: What did you do yesterday?

B: _____

2

A: What did you do yesterday?

B: _____

How Was Your Weekend?

Mini Talk Look and listen. ▶ 🎧94

Hi, Brad. How was your weekend?

It was great.

What did you do?

I visited the science museum.

CHECK 95

1 How was Brad's weekend? a ☐ b ☐

2 What did he do? a ☐ b ☐

Practice

(A) Listen and write the letter. 🎧 96   **(B)** Listen and repeat. 🎧 97

How was your weekend?   It was good.
I played at the park.

 played at the park ☐    joined a science camp ☐    baked bread ☐

 practiced the guitar ☐    watched a magic show ☐

 planted flowers ☐    painted a picture ☐    visited the palace ☐

Listen & Talk

A Listen and choose. 🎧 98

1

2

3

4

5

6

YOUR TURN

B Check and say.

How was your weekend?

It was fun. I _____.

cleaned my room

visited the palace

watched a magic show

Write & Talk

A Write, listen, and read. 🎧99

Joey: Mom, I'm home.

Mom: _____ was school today?

Joey: It was _____.

Mom: _____ did you do?

Joey: I _____ trees in the _____.

Mom: Sounds fun.

| good | garden | planted | How | What |

B Look and write. Then ask and answer.

What did you do yesterday?

How was it?

1 fun

2 good

3 great

baked cookies

painted a picture

joined a music camp

1 I _____. It was _____.

2 I _____. It was _____.

3 I _____. It was _____.

Reading

(A) Listen and read. 🎧 100

It's Jenny TV. I'm your friend, Jenny.

How was school today?

Was it good?

Here's a message from Roy.

It was a fun day.

I painted a big picture on the wall.

It was for the school concert.

I painted the music band.

My friends liked the picture. Look!

That's great!

(B) Circle or write.

1   Roy had a fun day.   (T / F)

2   He joined a music band.   (T / F)

3   What did he paint on the wall?

    ⋯⟶ He painted the _____.

Build Up

A Listen and repeat.  101

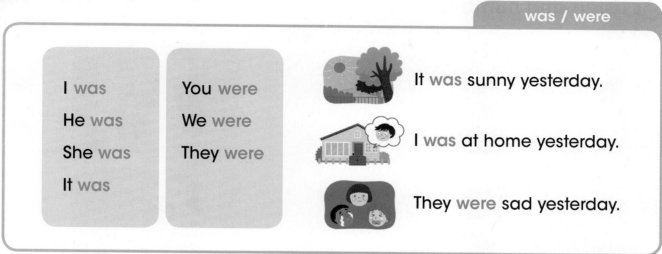

I was
He was
She was
It was

You were
We were
They were

It was sunny yesterday.

I was at home yesterday.

They were sad yesterday.

B Look and write.

1

It _____ rainy yesterday.

2

I _____ sick yesterday.

3

You _____ at the park yesterday.

4

He _____ at the library yesterday.

Check-Up

A Listen and number. 🎧102

B Listen and check. 🎧103

1

2

3

4

C Listen and choose. 🎧104

1 Susan _____ with Jane.

    ⓐ baked cookies   ⓑ painted a picture   ⓒ planted trees

2 Ron _____ on the weekend.

    ⓐ watched TV   ⓑ watched a movie   ⓒ watched a magic show

D Look and write.

1

A: _____ was your weekend?

B: It _____ good.

I _____ the guitar.

2

A: What _____ you do yesterday?

B: I _____ a picture.

It _____ great.

3

They _____ happy yesterday.

I _____ sad yesterday.

E Write and say.

1

A: How was your weekend?

B: _____ good.

_____

2

weekend

A: _____

B: It was great.

I _____.

Review 4

A Look and write.

> What did you do?   How was your weekend?   I watched a magic show.

Good morning, Bob.
_____

It was great.

_____

I joined a magic camp.

What did you do there?

_____
_____

Look.

?

!

Surprise!

Wow!

B Read and match.

1 How was your weekend? •

2 What did you do? •

3 What did you do at home? •

• I baked bread.

• I stayed home all day.

• It was okay.

C Read and write T or F.

1

A: How was your weekend?
B: It was good.
A: What did you do?
B: I listened to music.

2

A: What did you do yesterday?
B: I played at the park.
A: How was it?
B: It was fun.

3

A: What did you do yesterday?
B: I painted a picture.
A: How was it?
B: It was good.

Luna's Great Weekend

I go to the Animal Help Center on weekends.

My favorite animal is the dog.

I help the dogs there.

I wash the dogs.

I clean their houses.

I like to make toys for the dogs.

I like to make dog houses, too.

Today I'm making a new house for Toby.

"Toby, this house is yours. Do you like it?"

Toby likes the house.

1 This story is about _____.

ⓐ washing dogs   ⓑ helping dogs   ⓒ making houses

Comprehension

2 What does Luna do on weekends?

ⓐ She helps the dogs at the center.

ⓑ She goes shopping.

ⓒ She cleans the house.

3 Luna likes to _____.

ⓐ make dog houses   ⓑ help her mom   ⓒ play with dogs

4 What does Luna <u>not</u> do at the center?

ⓐ She washes the dogs.

ⓑ She cleans dog houses.

ⓒ She makes cookies.

Writing Practice

> What's your favorite animal? ⋯▸ My favorite animal is the dog.

1 What's your favorite sport?

⋯▸ My _____. (tennis)

2 What's your favorite fruit?

⋯▸ My _____. (the orange)

Mark's Summer Vacation 106

I'll go to New York again this summer.

My uncle lives there.

I visited him last winter. It was great!

We went to Broadway.

We watched a show together.

This time, we'll watch a baseball game.

I'll meet my favorite baseball player, Adam.

I'll take a picture with him.

I can't wait.

1   This story is about the boy's _____.

   ⓐ favorite sport   ⓑ trip to New York   ⓒ uncle in New York

Comprehension

2   What did the boy do last winter?

   ⓐ He played baseball.

   ⓑ He watched a show.

   ⓒ He visited the museum.

3   What will the boy do this summer?

   ⓐ He will visit his friend.

   ⓑ He will go to Broadway.

   ⓒ He will watch a baseball game.

4   The boy will _____ with Adam.

   ⓐ play baseball   ⓑ take a picture   ⓒ watch a show

Writing Practice

How was yesterday? ⋯▸ It was great. I visited my uncle.

1   How was your weekend?

   ⋯▸ It _____. I _____. (good / join a music camp)

2   How was school today?

   ⋯▸ It _____. I _____. (fun / plant flowers)

• **Present Simple**

verb + -s / -es / -ies					
bake	bakes		have	has	
bring	brings		help	helps	
buy	buys		make	makes	
catch	catches		meet	meets	
clean	cleans		paint	paints	
come	comes		play	plays	
cry	cries		read	reads	
dance	dances		ride	rides	
do	does		run	runs	
draw	draws		study	studies	
drink	drinks		take	takes	
eat	eats		teach	teaches	
finish	finishes		walk	walks	
fly	flies		wash	washes	
go	goes		watch	watches	

• Past Simple-Regular Verbs

verb+ -ed / -d					
arrive	arrived		open	opened	
bake	baked		paint	painted	
borrow	borrowed		pick	picked	
clean	cleaned		plant	planted	
climb	climbed		play	played	
cook	cooked		practice	practiced	
dance	danced		stay	stayed	
exercise	exercised		touch	touched	
help	helped		use	used	
join	joined		visit	visited	
jump	jumped		walk	walked	
learn	learned		wait	waited	
listen	listened		want	wanted	
look	looked		wash	washed	
move	moved		watch	watched	

Word List 4B

Unit 1　What Do You Do on Weekends?

bake bread　　　　　＿＿＿＿＿＿

clean my room　　　＿＿＿＿＿＿

fly a kite　　　　　＿＿＿＿＿＿

go swimming　　　　＿＿＿＿＿＿

go to the farm　　　＿＿＿＿＿＿

have soccer practice＿＿＿＿＿＿

on weekends　　　　＿＿＿＿＿＿

read books　　　　　＿＿＿＿＿＿

ride my bike　　　　＿＿＿＿＿＿

study English　　　＿＿＿＿＿＿

take a dance class　＿＿＿＿＿＿

wash my dog　　　　＿＿＿＿＿＿

watch sports　　　　＿＿＿＿＿＿

Unit 2　How Many Balloons Do You Have?

apple pie　　　　　＿＿＿＿＿＿

bottle　　　　　　　＿＿＿＿＿＿

box　　　　　　　　＿＿＿＿＿＿

candle　　　　　　　＿＿＿＿＿＿

crayon　　　　　　　＿＿＿＿＿＿

cupcake　　　　　　＿＿＿＿＿＿

donut　　　　　　　＿＿＿＿＿＿

fork　　　　　　　　＿＿＿＿＿＿

party hat　　　　　＿＿＿＿＿＿

plate　　　　　　　＿＿＿＿＿＿

scissors　　　　　　＿＿＿＿＿＿

spoon　　　　　　　＿＿＿＿＿＿

tape　　　　　　　　＿＿＿＿＿＿

Unit 3　May I Come In?

borrow your pen　　＿＿＿＿＿＿

bring my dog　　　　＿＿＿＿＿＿

come in　　　　　　＿＿＿＿＿＿

drink some juice　　＿＿＿＿＿＿

eat on the bus　　　＿＿＿＿＿＿

eat some snacks　　＿＿＿＿＿＿

go to the restroom　＿＿＿＿＿＿

make a library card＿＿＿＿＿＿

sit here　　　　　　＿＿＿＿＿＿

take pictures　　　＿＿＿＿＿＿

touch this car　　　＿＿＿＿＿＿

use my phone　　　＿＿＿＿＿＿

use the computer　　＿＿＿＿＿＿

Unit 4　My Favorite Subject Is Music

draw pictures　　　＿＿＿＿＿＿

drink milk　　　　　＿＿＿＿＿＿

favorite subject　　＿＿＿＿＿＿

listen to music　　＿＿＿＿＿＿

play basketball　　＿＿＿＿＿＿

play sports　　　　＿＿＿＿＿＿

play the drums　　　＿＿＿＿＿＿

read maps　　　　　＿＿＿＿＿＿

read science books＿＿＿＿＿＿

sing songs　　　　　＿＿＿＿＿＿

speak English　　　＿＿＿＿＿＿

study math　　　　　＿＿＿＿＿＿

watch the stars　　＿＿＿＿＿＿

Unit 5   We'll Make Cookies Tomorrow

catch fish   _____

catch fireflies   _____

fly a drone   _____

go to the river   _____

go to the water park   _____

have a picnic   _____

have a violin lesson   _____

make cookies   _____

meet Nick   _____

pick apples   _____

plant trees   _____

play games   _____

play in the water   _____

Unit 6   What Will You Do This Summer?

go hiking   _____

go on a trip   _____

go to the beach   _____

join a Christmas party   _____

join a summer camp   _____

learn Chinese   _____

meet koalas   _____

read many books   _____

ride a boat   _____

swim at the beach   _____

take swimming lessons   _____

visit my grandparents   _____

visit the art museum   _____

Unit 7   What Did You Do Yesterday?

cleaned my room   _____

cleaned the windows   _____

did my homework   _____

helped my dad   _____

listened to music   _____

played badminton   _____

played computer games   _____

stayed home all day   _____

visited my aunt   _____

washed his car   _____

watched a basketball game   _____

watched a movie   _____

Unit 8   How Was Your Weekend?

baked bread   _____

joined a science camp   _____

painted a picture   _____

painted ~ on the wall   _____

planted flowers   _____

played at the park   _____

practiced the guitar   _____

visited the palace   _____

visited the science museum   _____

was/were at home   _____

watched a magic show   _____

Syllabus 4B

Unit 1 What Do You Do on Weekends?

Structures	Vocabulary		Grammar
• What do you do on weekends? I take a dance class. • What about you? • What do you do there? • I have soccer practice on Saturdays.	bake bread clean my room go to the farm have soccer practice read books	ride my bike wash my dog watch sports	-s, -es, -ies
			Reading

Unit 2 How Many Balloons Do You Have?

Structures	Vocabulary			Grammar

• Do you have balloons?
  Yes, I do.
• How many balloons do you have(need, want)?
  I have(need, want) five balloons.
	apple pie
	candle
	cupcake
	donut
	fork
	party hat
		plate
		spoon
		bottle
		box
		crayon
		scissors
			tape
			kiwi
			orange
			strawberry
				How many ~?

				Reading

Review 1

Unit 3 May I Come In?

Structures	Vocabulary		Grammar

• May I come in?
  Yes, you may. / No, you may not.
• Can I sit here?
  Yes, you can. / No, you can't.
• You can't bring your dog.
• You may not bring animals.
	borrow your pen
	bring my dog
	come in
	drink some juice
	go to the restroom
	sit here
		use my phone
		use the computer
		eat on the bus
		take pictures
		touch this car
			May I ~?
			Can I ~?

			Reading

Unit 4 My Favorite Subject Is Music

Structures	Vocabulary		Grammar

• What's your favorite subject?
  My favorite subject is music.
• Do you like to sing songs?
  Yes, I do. / No, I don't.
• I like to play the drums.
	art
	English
	math
	music
	P.E.
	science
	social studies
		draw pictures
		speak English
		study math
		sing songs
		play sports
		read science books
		read maps
			like to, likes to

			Reading

Review 2

Unit 5 We'll Make Cookies Tomorrow

Structures	Vocabulary		Grammar
• We'll(I'll) make cookies tomorrow. • Can you join us(me)? Sure. / Sorry, I can't.	catch fish go to the water park have a picnic make cookies	meet Nick pick apples plant trees play games	will
			Reading

Unit 6 What Will You Do This Summer?

Structures	Vocabulary		Grammar

• What will you do this summer?
  I'll go to the beach.
 • What will you do there?
  I'll ride a boat.
 • Have a good time.
  You, too.
	go on a trip
	 go to the beach
	 join a summer camp
	 learn Chinese
		read many books
		 take swimming lessons
		 visit my grandparents
		 visit the art museum
			What will ~?

			Reading
Review 3			

Unit 7 What Did You Do Yesterday?

Structures	Vocabulary		Grammar
• What did you do yesterday? I played computer games.	cleaned my room helped my dad listened to music played badminton stayed home	visited my aunt watched a movie did my homework played computer games	-ed
			Reading

Unit 8 How Was Your Weekend?

Structures	Vocabulary		Grammar

• How was your weekend?
  It was good(fun, great).
  I visited the science museum.
	baked bread
	 joined a science camp
	 painted a picture
	 planted flowers
		played at the park
		 practiced the guitar
		 visited the palace
		 watched a magic show
			was, were

			Reading
Review 4			

Midterm TEST 4B

Institute

Name

Score   /100

[1-2] Listen and choose.
잘 듣고, 그림에 알맞지 않은 것을 고르세요.

1 ⓐ 　　ⓑ

ⓒ 　　ⓓ

2 ⓐ 　　ⓑ

ⓒ 　　ⓓ

[3-4] Listen and choose.
잘 듣고, 그림에 알맞은 것을 고르세요.

3 　　ⓐ　ⓑ　ⓒ　ⓓ

4 　　ⓐ　ⓑ　ⓒ　ⓓ

5 Listen and mark ○ or ✕.
잘 듣고 그림에 알맞으면 ○ 표, 그렇지 않으면 ✕ 표 하세요.

(   )

[6-7] Listen and choose.
잘 듣고, 알맞은 응답을 고르세요.

6 ⓐ　　　ⓑ　　　ⓒ　　　ⓓ

7 ⓐ　　　ⓑ　　　ⓒ　　　ⓓ

[8-9] Listen and choose.
잘 듣고, 알맞은 것을 고르세요.

8 ⓐ 　　ⓑ

ⓒ 　　ⓓ

9 ⓐ 　　ⓑ

ⓒ 　　ⓓ

10 Listen and choose.
잘 듣고, 그림에 알맞은 것을 고르세요.

　　ⓐ　　ⓑ　　ⓒ　　ⓓ

[11-12] Look and choose.
그림을 보고 알맞은 것을 고르세요.

11

ⓐ I ride my bike on Sundays.
ⓑ I fly a drone on Fridays.
ⓒ I go to the farm on Mondays.
ⓓ I have soccer practice on Saturdays.

12

ⓐ He likes to read books.
ⓑ He likes to draw pictures.
ⓒ He likes to play sports.
ⓓ He likes to study science.

13 Read and choose.
대화를 읽고 알맞은 그림을 고르세요.

A: May I use my phone here?
B: No, you may not.

ⓐ    ⓑ

ⓒ    ⓓ

[14-15] Unscramble.
단어를 배열하여 문장을 완성하세요.

14

_____?
(have / How many / do / you / forks)

15

_____?
(do / on / What / you / weekends / do)

16 Read and choose.
대화의 빈칸에 알맞지 않은 것을 고르세요.

A: May I go to the restroom?
B: _____

ⓐ Sure.   ⓑ Yes, you may.
ⓒ No, you may not.   ⓓ Sorry, I can't.

17 Read and choose.
대화의 빈칸에 알맞은 것을 고르세요.

A: What do you do on Saturdays?
B: I go to the park.
A: _____
B: I ride my bike.

ⓐ Can I go to the park?
ⓑ What do you do there?
ⓒ What about you?
ⓓ Do you like to ride a bike?

18 Put the sentences in the order.
문장을 바르게 배열하여 대화를 만드세요.

ⓐ Yes, I do.
ⓑ Do you have spoons?
ⓒ I have ten spoons.
ⓓ How many spoons do you have?

(   ) → (   ) → (   ) → (   )

[19-20] Look and write.
그림을 보고 빈칸에 알맞은 말을 쓰세요.

19

My favorite subject is _____.

I like to _____.

20

A: May I _____ your _____?

B: Yes, _____ _____.

Final TEST 4B

Institute _____

Name _____

Score _____ /100

[1-2] Listen and choose.
잘 듣고, 그림에 알맞은 것을 고르세요.

1  ⓐ   ⓑ   ⓒ   ⓓ

2  ⓐ   ⓑ   ⓒ   ⓓ

[3-4] Listen and choose.
잘 듣고, 알맞은 응답을 고르세요.

3 ⓐ   ⓑ   ⓒ   ⓓ

4 ⓐ   ⓑ   ⓒ   ⓓ

[5-7] Listen and choose.
잘 듣고, 알맞은 것을 고르세요.

5 ⓐ  ⓑ

ⓒ  ⓓ

6 ⓐ  ⓑ

ⓒ  ⓓ

7 ⓐ  ⓑ

ⓒ  ⓓ

8 Listen and choose.
잘 듣고, 이어질 응답으로 알맞지 않은 것을 고르세요.

ⓐ   ⓑ   ⓒ   ⓓ

9 Listen and choose.
잘 듣고, 내용에 알맞은 것을 고르세요.

ⓐ They will make cookies.

ⓑ They will have a picnic.

ⓒ They will go to the water park.

ⓓ They will visit the art museum.

10 Listen and choose.
잘 듣고, 어색한 대화를 고르세요.

ⓐ   ⓑ   ⓒ   ⓓ

[11-12] Read and write the letter.
문장을 읽고 알맞은 것을 골라 기호를 쓰세요.

ⓑ
ⓒ ⓓ

11
I played games yesterday.

( )

12
I watched a magic show yesterday.

( )

13 Look and choose.
그림을 보고 알맞은 것을 고르세요.

ⓐ I'll plant trees.
ⓑ I'll pick apples.
ⓒ I'll go to the beach.
ⓓ I'll make apple pies.

14 Read and choose.
대화의 빈칸에 알맞은 것을 고르세요.

A: What did he do yesterday?
B: _____

ⓐ He visits his aunt.
ⓑ He plays at the park.
ⓒ He painted a picture.
ⓓ He will join a science camp.

[15-16] Read and write.
대화의 빈칸에 공통으로 알맞은 말을 쓰세요.

15
A: How _____ your weekend?
B: It _____ good.

16
A: What _____ you do this winter?
B: I _____ learn Chinese.

17 Put the sentences in the order.
문장을 바르게 배열하여 대화를 만드세요.

ⓐ I'll go on a trip.
ⓑ I'll go hiking. How about you?
ⓒ What will you do this weekend?
ⓓ Sounds great. Have a good time.

( ) → ( ) → ( ) → ( )

18 Read and choose.
대화를 읽고 어색한 것을 고르세요.

ⓐ A: How was school today?
   B: I planted flowers in the garden.
ⓑ A: What did you do yesterday?
   B: I baked bread with Mom.
ⓒ A: What will you do this summer?
   B: I'll take swimming lessons.
ⓓ A: I'll visit the palace tomorrow.
    Can you join me?
   B: Sure.

[19-20] Look and write.
그림을 보고 빈칸에 알맞은 말을 쓰세요.

19

A: _____ did you do yesterday?
B: I _____ home all day. I _____ TV.

20

A: _____ will you do this summer?
B: We _____ _____ _____.

LET'S GO
2nd Edition
to the English World

4B

2nd Edition

LET'S GO

to the English World

4B

Word Book
& Workbook

CHUNJAE EDUCATION, INC.

Word Book

What Do You Do on Weekends?

Ⓐ Listen and repeat. 🎧01 🎧02

watch sports 운동 경기를 보다	**I watch sports on Saturdays.** 나는 토요일마다 운동 경기를 봐.
read books 책을 읽다	**I read books on weekends.** 나는 주말마다 책을 읽어.
bake bread 빵을 굽다	**He bakes bread on Mondays.** 그는 월요일마다 빵을 구워.
go to the farm 농장에 가다	**She goes to the farm on Sundays.** 그녀는 일요일마다 농장에 가.
have soccer practice 축구 연습을 하다	**We have soccer practice on Fridays.** 우리는 금요일마다 축구 연습을 해.
ride my bike 내 자전거를 타다	**I ride my bike on Wednesdays.** 나는 수요일마다 내 자전거를 타.
clean my room 내 방을 청소하다	**I clean my room every day.** 나는 매일 내 방을 청소해.
wash my dog 내 개를 씻기다[목욕시키다]	**I wash my dog on Thursdays.** 나는 목요일마다 내 개를 목욕시켜.

B Read, write, and say.

1 watch sports
운동 경기를 보다

_____ _____ _____

2 read books
책을 읽다

_____ _____ _____

3 bake bread
빵을 굽다

_____ _____ _____

4 go to the farm
농장에 가다

_____ _____ _____

5 have soccer practice
축구 연습을 하다

_____ _____ _____

6 ride my bike
내 자전거를 타다

_____ _____ _____

7 clean my room
내 방을 청소하다

_____ _____ _____

8 wash my dog
내 개를 목욕시키다

_____ _____ _____

Learn More

weekend 주말	**on Wednesdays** 수요일마다	**on Saturdays** 토요일마다
on Mondays 월요일마다	**on Thursdays** 목요일마다	**on Sundays** 일요일마다
on Tuesdays 화요일마다	**on Fridays** 금요일마다	

A Listen and repeat. 14 15

cupcake 컵케이크	**How many** cupcakes **do you have?** 너는 몇 개의 컵케이크를 가지고 있니?
apple pie 사과파이	**How many** apple pies **do you have?** 너는 몇 개의 사과파이를 가지고 있니?
donut 도넛	**How many** donuts **do you want?** 너는 몇 개의 도넛을 원하니?
plate 접시	**How many** plates **do you need?** 너는 몇 개의 접시가 필요하니?
fork 포크	**I have two** forks. 나는 두 개의 포크를 가지고 있어.
spoon 숟가락	**She has five** spoons. 그녀는 다섯 개의 숟가락을 가지고 있어.
candle 초	**We need ten** candles. 우리는 열 개의 초가 필요해.
party hat 파티 모자	**Do you have** party hats? 너는 파티 모자를 가지고 있니?

Read, write, and say.

1 cupcake
컵케이크

_____ _____ _____

2 apple pie
사과파이

_____ _____ _____

3 donut
도넛

_____ _____ _____

4 plate
접시

_____ _____ _____

5 fork
포크

_____ _____ _____

6 spoon
숟가락

_____ _____ _____

7 candle
초

_____ _____ _____

8 party hat
파티 모자

_____ _____ _____

Learn More

balloon 풍선(balloons)　　**box** 상자(boxes)　　**paper** 종이(셀 수 없는 물건)

cookie 쿠키(cookies)　　**crayon** 크레용(crayons)　　**tape** 테이프(셀 수 없는 물건)

scissors 가위(복수형 단어)　　**bottle** 병(bottles)

Ⓐ **Listen and repeat.** 27 28

drink some juice 주스를 좀 마시다	**May I** drink some juice **here?** 여기서 주스를 좀 마셔도 되나요?
use my phone 내 전화를 사용하다	**May I** use my phone**?** 제 전화를 사용해도 되나요?
use the computer 컴퓨터를 사용하다	**May I** use the computer**?** 컴퓨터를 사용해도 되나요?
borrow your pen 네 펜을 빌리다	**May I** borrow your pen**?** 당신의 펜을 빌려도 되나요?
come in 들어가다	**May I** come in**?** 들어가도 되나요?
go to the restroom 화장실에 가다	**Can I** go to the restroom**?** 화장실에 가도 되나요?
sit here 여기에 앉다	**Can I** sit here**?** 여기에 앉아도 되나요?
bring my dog 내 개를 데려오다	**Can I** bring my dog**?** 제 개를 데려와도 되나요?

B Read, write, and say.

☐ Read ☐ Write ☐ Say

1 drink some juice
주스를 좀 마시다

_____ _____ _____

2 use my phone
내 전화를 사용하다

_____ _____ _____

3 use the computer
컴퓨터를 사용하다

_____ _____ _____

4 borrow your pen
네 펜을 빌리다

_____ _____ _____

5 come in
들어가다

_____ _____ _____

6 go to the restroom
화장실에 가다

_____ _____ _____

7 sit here
여기에 앉다

_____ _____ _____

8 bring my dog
내 개를 데려오다

_____ _____ _____

Learn More

here 여기에서	May I drink some juice here? 여기에서 주스를 좀 마셔도 되나요?
inside 안에서	You can't eat inside. 안에서 먹을 수 없어요.
outside 밖에서	You can use your phone outside. 밖에서 전화를 사용할 수 있어요.

My Favorite Subject Is Music

favorite subject 가장 좋아하는 과목	**My** favorite subject **is English.** 내가 가장 좋아하는 과목은 영어야.
study math 수학을 공부하다	**I like to** study math**.** 나는 수학 공부하는 것을 좋아해.
speak English 영어를 말하다	**I like to** speak English**.** 나는 영어를 말하는 것을 좋아해.
sing songs 노래를 부르다	**They like to** sing songs**.** 그들은 노래 부르는 것을 좋아해.
draw pictures 그림을 그리다	**She likes to** draw pictures**.** 그녀는 그림 그리는 것을 좋아해.
read maps 지도를 읽다	**He likes to** read maps**.** 그는 지도 읽는 것을 좋아해.
play sports 운동 경기를 하다	**Do you like to** play sports**?** 너는 운동 경기 하는 것을 좋아하니?
read science books 과학책을 읽다	**Do you like to** read science books**?** 너는 과학책 읽는 것을 좋아하니?

B Read, write, and say.

☐ Read ☐ Write ☐ Say

1 favorite subject
가장 좋아하는 과목

2 study math
수학을 공부하다

3 speak English
영어를 말하다

4 sing songs
노래를 부르다

5 draw pictures
그림을 그리다

6 read maps
지도를 읽다

7 play sports
운동 경기를 하다

8 read science books
과학책을 읽다

Learn More

social studies 사회	art 미술	watch the stars 별을 보다
math 수학	P.E. 체육	bake cookies 쿠키를 굽다
music 음악	science 과학	play the drums 북을 치다

UNIT 5 We'll Make Cookies Tomorrow

A **Listen and repeat.** 53 54

make cookies 쿠키를 만들다	**I'll** make cookies **tomorrow.** 나는 내일 쿠키를 만들 거야.
pick apples 사과를 따다	**He'll** pick apples **tomorrow.** 그는 내일 사과를 딸 거야.
plant trees 나무를 심다	**I'll** plant trees **this weekend.** 나는 이번 주말에 나무를 심을 거야.
catch fish 물고기를 잡다	**She'll** catch fish **this weekend.** 그녀는 이번 주말에 물고기를 잡을 거야.
meet Nick 닉을 만나다	**I'll** meet Nick **this Sunday.** 나는 이번 일요일에 닉을 만날 거야.
have a picnic 소풍을 가다	**We'll** have a picnic **this afternoon.** 우리는 오늘 오후에 소풍을 갈 거야.
play games 게임을 하다	**I'll** play games **today.** 나는 오늘 게임을 할 거야.
go to the water park 워터파크에 가다	**They'll** go to the water park **today.** 그들은 오늘 워터파크에 갈 거야.

10

B Read, write, and say.

□ Read □ Write □ Say

1 make cookies
쿠키를 만들다

_____ _____ _____

2 pick apples
사과를 따다

_____ _____ _____

3 plant trees
나무를 심다

_____ _____ _____

4 catch fish
물고기를 잡다

_____ _____ _____

5 meet Nick
닉을 만나다

_____ _____ _____

6 have a picnic
소풍을 가다

_____ _____ _____

7 play games
게임을 하다

_____ _____ _____

8 go to the water park
워터파크에 가다

_____ _____ _____

Learn More

tomorrow 내일	I'll meet friends tomorrow. 나는 내일 친구들을 만날 거야.
this 이번	I'll bake bread this weekend. 나는 이번 주말에 빵을 구울 거야.
afternoon 오후	In the afternoon, we will go to the river. 오후에 우리는 강에 갈 거야.
join 함께하다	Can you join me? 나와 함께할래?

What Will You Do This Summer?

Ⓐ **Listen and repeat.** 66 67

go on a trip 여행을 가다	**I'll** go on a trip **to Sydney.** 나는 시드니로 여행을 갈 거야.
go to the beach 해변에 가다	**We'll** go to the beach **this summer.** 우리는 이번 여름에 해변에 갈 거야.
visit my grandparents 조부모님을 방문하다	**I'll** visit my grandparents **this weekend.** 나는 이번 주말에 조부모님을 방문할 거야.
visit the art museum 미술관을 방문하다	**She'll** visit the art museum **tomorrow.** 그녀는 내일 미술관을 방문할 거야.
learn Chinese 중국어를 배우다	**He'll** learn Chinese **this winter.** 그는 이번 겨울에 중국어를 배울 거야.
read many books 많은 책을 읽다	**I'll** read many books **at home.** 나는 집에서 많은 책을 읽을 거야.
take swimming lessons 수영 레슨을 받다	**He'll** take swimming lessons **this summer.** 그는 이번 여름에 수영 레슨을 받을 거야.
join a summer camp 여름 캠프에 참가하다	**They'll** join a summer camp. 그들은 여름 캠프에 참가할 거야.

B Read, write, and say.

1 go on a trip
여행을 가다

_____ _____ _____

2 go to the beach
해변에 가다

_____ _____ _____

3 visit my grandparents
조부모님을 방문하다

_____ _____ _____

4 visit the art museum
미술관을 방문하다

_____ _____ _____

5 learn Chinese
중국어를 배우다

_____ _____ _____

6 read many books
많은 책을 읽다

_____ _____ _____

7 take swimming lessons
수영 레슨을 받다

_____ _____ _____

8 join a summer camp
여름 캠프에 참가하다

_____ _____ _____

Learn More

this summer 이번 여름	**I'll go to the sea** this summer. 나는 이번 여름에 바다에 갈 거야.
this winter 이번 겨울	**What will you do** this winter? 너는 이번 겨울에 무엇을 할 거니?
take pictures 사진을 찍다	**I'll** take funny pictures. 나는 웃긴 사진들을 찍을 거야.
ride a boat 보트를 타다	**I'll** ride a boat. 나는 보트를 탈 거야.

UNIT 7 What Did You Do Yesterday?

A Listen and repeat. 79 80

listened to music 음악을 들었다	I listened to music **yesterday.** 나는 어제 음악을 들었어.
cleaned my room 내 방을 청소했다	I cleaned my room **yesterday.** 나는 어제 내 방을 청소했어.
visited my aunt 이모를 방문했다	I visited my aunt **yesterday.** 나는 어제 이모를 방문했어.
stayed home 집에 머물렀다	**He** stayed home **all day.** 그는 하루 종일 집에 있었어.
helped my dad 아빠를 도왔다	I helped my dad **yesterday.** 나는 어제 아빠를 도왔어.
played badminton 배드민턴을 쳤다	**They** played badminton **together.** 그들은 함께 배드민턴을 쳤어.
watched a movie 영화를 봤다	**We** watched a movie **in the evening.** 우리는 저녁에 영화를 봤어.

1 listened to music
음악을 들었다

_____ _____ _____

2 cleaned my room
내 방을 청소했다

_____ _____ _____

3 visited my aunt
이모를 방문했다

_____ _____ _____

4 stayed home
집에 머물렀다

_____ _____ _____

5 helped my dad
아빠를 도왔다

_____ _____ _____

6 played badminton
배드민턴을 쳤다

_____ _____ _____

7 watched a movie
영화를 봤다

_____ _____ _____

Learn More

all day 하루 종일	**I stayed home** all day. 나는 하루 종일 집에 있었어.
played computer games 컴퓨터 게임을 했다	**I** played computer games **with friends.** 나는 친구들과 컴퓨터 게임을 했어.
did my homework 숙제를 했다	**I** did my homework **yesterday.** 나는 어제 숙제를 했어.
washed his car 그의 자동차를 세차했다	**He** washed his car **last weekend.** 그는 지난 주말에 그의 자동차를 세차했어.

A Listen and repeat.

played at the park 공원에서 놀았다	**I** played at the park **yesterday.** 나는 어제 공원에서 놀았어.
joined a science camp 과학 캠프에 참가했다	**She** joined a science camp**.** 그녀는 과학 캠프에 참가했어.
baked bread 빵을 구웠다	**He** baked bread **with Mom.** 그는 엄마와 빵을 구웠어.
practiced the guitar 기타를 연습했다	**I** practiced the guitar **at home.** 나는 집에서 기타를 연습했어.
watched a magic show 마술 쇼를 봤다	**They** watched a magic show **yesterday.** 그들은 어제 마술 쇼를 봤어.
planted flowers 꽃을 심었다	**We** planted flowers **yesterday.** 우리는 어제 꽃을 심었어.
painted a picture 그림을 그렸다	**I** painted a picture **at home.** 나는 집에서 그림을 그렸어.
visited the palace 궁전을 방문했다	**My family** visited the palace **yesterday.** 우리 가족은 어제 궁전을 방문했어.

1 played at the park
공원에서 놀았다

_____ _____ _____

2 joined a science camp
과학 캠프에 참가했다

_____ _____ _____

3 baked bread
빵을 구웠다

_____ _____ _____

4 practiced the guitar
기타를 연습했다

_____ _____ _____

5 watched a magic show
마술 쇼를 봤다

_____ _____ _____

6 planted flowers
꽃을 심었다

_____ _____ _____

7 painted a picture
그림을 그렸다

_____ _____ _____

8 visited the palace
궁전을 방문했다

_____ _____ _____

Learn More

garden 정원	I planted trees in the garden. 나는 정원에 나무를 심었어.
message 메시지	Here's a message from Roy. 여기 로이에게서 온 메시지가 있어요.
wall 벽	I painted a picture on the wall. 나는 벽에 그림을 그렸어.
concert 콘서트	It was for the school concert. 그것은 학교 콘서트를 위한 거였어.

Workbook

What Do You Do on Weekends?

Words

A Look and write.

| bake bread | ride my bike | wash my dog | clean my room |

1

2

3

4

_____   _____   _____   _____

B Look and check.

1

☐ I watch movies.

☐ I watch sports.

2

☐ I read books.

☐ I help my mom.

3

☐ I go to the farm.

☐ I play with friends.

4

☐ I take a robot class.

☐ I have soccer practice.

Practice

A Circle and write.

1  I (watch sports / play basketball) on weekends.

_____

2  I (clean my room / read books) on weekends.

_____

3  I (go to the farm / ride my bike) on weekends.

_____

B Read and match.

1
A: What do you do on weekends?
B: I ride my bike.

•  ⓐ

2
A: What do you do on weekends?
B: I bake bread.

•  ⓑ

3
A: What do you do on weekends?
B: I have soccer practice.

•  ⓒ

4
A: What do you do on weekends?
B: I wash my dog.

•  ⓓ

Write & Talk

Ⓐ Read and write T or F.

1

A: What do you do on Tuesdays?

B: I bake bread.

2

A: What do you do on Mondays?

B: I go to the farm.

3

A: What does she do on Sundays?

B: She has soccer practice.

4

A: What does he do on Fridays?

B: He cleans his room.

Ⓑ Read, choose, and write.

A: **1** _____

B: I usually go to the farm.

A: **2** _____

B: I help my uncle.

A: Sounds good.

B: **3** _____

A: I have soccer practice on Saturdays.

ⓐ What do you do there?

ⓑ What about you?

ⓒ What do you do on Saturdays?

Reading

A Read and write.

Jane _____ to the library on Saturdays.

She reads _____ there.

She watches movies, too.

Tom _____ his room on weekends.

And he washes _____.

He _____ bread with Mom, too.

He's busy on _____.

| weekends | goes | bakes | his dog | cleans | many books |

B Look and choose.

1

What do you do on Wednesdays?

ⓐ I go to the park.

ⓑ I ride my bike.

2

What does she do on weekends?

ⓐ She cleans her room.

ⓑ She watches sports.

3

What does he do on Saturdays?

ⓐ He takes a robot class.

ⓑ He has soccer practice.

Build Up

Ⓐ Read and circle.

1 He (play / **plays**) with friends on weekends.

2 Kate (**cleans** / cleanes) her room on Mondays.

3 My sister (**goes** / go) hiking on Wednesdays.

4 Dad (watchs / **watches**) sports on Sundays.

Ⓑ Change and write.

1  She _____ a kite on weekends.

2  He _____ cookies on Saturdays.

3  Alice _____ her dog on Sundays.

4  My brother _____ English on Mondays.

| bake |
| wash |
| fly |
| study |

Writing

Ⓐ Make the sentence.

1 _____

(do / weekends / What / on / do / you / ?) 너는 주말마다 무엇을 하니?

2 _____

(on / does / Fridays / do / What / Sam / ?) 샘은 금요일마다 무엇을 하니?

3 _____

(What / they / on / do / Tuesdays / do / ?) 그들은 화요일마다 무엇을 하니?

4 _____

(on / books / weekends / read / I / .) 나는 주말마다 책을 읽어.

5 _____

(Saturdays / to the farm / on / goes / Jane / .) 제인은 토요일마다 농장에 가.

6 _____

(his bike / on / Tom / rides / Sundays / .) 톰은 일요일마다 자전거를 타.

7 _____

(I / on / soccer practice / have / Mondays / .) 나는 월요일마다 축구 연습을 해.

How Many Balloons Do You Have?

Words

A Look and write the letter.

@ six donuts	ⓑ four forks	ⓒ six spoons
ⓓ ten candles	ⓔ eight plates	ⓕ seven cupcakes

1

2

3

4

5

6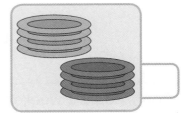

B Circle and write.

1

I have _____.

(six cupcakes / two apple pies)

2

I have _____.

(three party hats / four plates)

3

I have _____.

(eight forks / five spoons)

Practice

Ⓐ Circle and choose.

1

How many (spoons / forks) do you have?

ⓐ I have three spoons.　ⓑ I have two forks.

2

How many (cupcakes / apple pies) do you have?

ⓐ I have five cupcakes.　ⓑ I have five apple pies.

3

How many (candles / plates) do you have?

ⓐ I have four candles.　ⓑ I have six plates.

Ⓑ Match and write.

1

A: How many party hats do you have?

B: I have ＿＿＿＿＿ ＿＿＿＿＿＿.

ⓐ

2

A: How many spoons do you have?

B: I have ＿＿＿＿＿ ＿＿＿＿＿＿.

ⓑ

3

A: How many donuts do you have?

B: I have ＿＿＿＿＿ ＿＿＿＿＿＿.

ⓒ

Write & Talk

A Look and write.

1

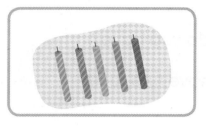

A: How many candles do you have?

B: I have _____ _____.

2

A: _____ _____ cupcakes do you _____?

B: I need _____ _____.

3

A: _____ _____ _____ do we need?

B: _____ _____ _____ balloons.

B Read and match.

1 How many donuts do you have? •   • We have eight plates.

2 How many forks do you need? •   • I need four forks.

3 How many plates do we have? •   • I have six donuts.

4 How many apple pies do we need? •   • We need ten apple pies.

Reading

(A) Read, choose, and write.

Let's make a green car.

1 _____

We have boxes, bottles, and paper plates.

2 _____

We have four plates.

3 _____

We need crayons, scissors, and tape.

I have crayons.

4 _____

Yes, she does. She has tape, too.

ⓐ Does Tina have scissors?

ⓑ What do we have?

ⓒ How many plates do we have?

ⓓ What do we need?

(B) Read and write.

1

Ben: Let's make a house.
Ann: What do you have?
Ben: I have two boxes.

What does Ben have?

···▸ He _____ _____ _____.

2

Mike: Let's draw a plane.
Kate: What do we need?
Mike: We need crayons.
Kate: I have ten crayons.

How many crayons does Kate have?

···▸ She _____ _____ _____.

Build Up

(A) Write and match.

1

A: _____ do you have?

B: I have five cupcakes.

ⓐ

2

A: _____ do you want?

B: I want four donuts.

ⓑ

3

A: _____ do you need?

B: I need three forks.

ⓒ

4

A: _____ do you have?

B: I have two robots.

ⓓ

5

A: _____ do we need?

B: We need six plates.

ⓔ

6

A: _____ do you want?

B: I want two cookies.

ⓕ

A Make the sentence.

1 _____

(do / cupcakes / How many / have / you / ?) 너는 몇 개의 컵케이크를 가지고 있니?

2 _____

(plates / How many / need / you / do / ?) 너는 몇 개의 접시가 필요하니?

3 _____

(do / you / many / How / candles / want / ?) 너는 몇 개의 초를 원하니?

4 _____

(have / I / spoons / ten / .) 나는 열 개의 숟가락을 가지고 있어.

5 _____

(party hats / has / She / eight / .) 그녀는 여덟 개의 파티 모자를 가지고 있어.

6 _____

(donuts / want / I / six / .) 나는 여섯 개의 도넛을 원해.

7 _____

(three / need / candles / We / .) 우리는 세 개의 초가 필요해.

May I Come In?

Words

A Look and match.

1  **2** **3** **4**

sit here

come in

drink some juice

go to the restroom

B Look and circle.

1

May I
use the computer
use my phone
?

2

May I
bring my dog
walk my dog
?

3

May I
watch TV
use the computer
?

4

May I
borrow your pen
sit here
?

Practice

A Look and write.

come in	borrow your pen	sit here	bring my dog

1

May I _____ ?

2

May I _____ ?

3

May I _____ ?

4

May I _____ ?

B Read, number, and choose.

1 May I go to the restroom?　　ⓐ Yes, you may.　　ⓑ No, you may not.

2 May I drink some juice?　　ⓐ Yes, you may.　　ⓑ No, you may not.

3 May I use the computer?　　ⓐ Yes, you may.　　ⓑ No, you may not.

4 May I use my phone?　　ⓐ Yes, you may.　　ⓑ No, you may not.

Write & Talk

A Look, read, and write T or F.

1 　2 　3 　4

1
A: May I go to the restroom?
B: No, you may not. ☐

2
A: May I bring my dog?
B: Yes, you may. ☐

3
A: May I use the computer?
B: Sure. ☐

4
A: May I come in?
B: Yes, you may. ☐

B Unscramble and match.

1
A: May _____?
(take / I / pictures)
B: No, you may not. •

2
A: May _____?
(I / my / dog / bring)
B: Yes, you may. •

3
A: May _____?
(use / my / I / phone)
B: No, you may not. •

34

Reading

A Read, choose, and write the letter.

1 Q: May I borrow books?

A: Yes, you may. _____

2 Q: May I bring my hamster?

A: No, you may not. _____

3 Q: May I use my phone?

A: No, you may not. _____

4 Q: May I use the computer here?

A: Yes, you may. _____

ⓐ We have ten computers.

ⓑ You can't bring animals in the library.

ⓒ You can use it outside.

ⓓ Please make a library card.

B Look and write.

1 No

2 Yes

3 Yes

4 No

1

A: May I _____?

B: _____

2

A: May I _____?

B: _____

3

A: May I _____?

B: _____

4

A: May I _____?

B: _____

Build Up

A Look and write.

eat	touch	borrow	go	take

1

A: _____ your eraser?

B: _____, you can.

2

A: _____ some snacks?

B: _____, you may not.

3

A: _____ to the restroom?

B: _____, you may.

4

A: _____ a picture?

B: _____, you may not.

5

A: _____ this car?

B: _____, you may not.

Writing

Ⓐ Make the sentence.

1 _____

(come / May / in / I / ?) 들어가도 되나요?

2 _____

(here / some juice / drink / I / May / ?) 여기서 주스를 좀 마셔도 되나요?

3 _____

(I / May / my phone / use / ?) 제 전화를 써도 되나요?

4 _____

(You / animals / may not / the library / in / bring / .)
도서관에는 동물들을 데려오면 안 됩니다.

5 _____

(can't / eat / You / the bus / on / .) 버스에서는 먹을 수 없어요.

6 _____

(use / Can / the computer / I / ?) 컴퓨터를 사용해도 되나요?

7 _____

(go / to / I / May / the restroom / ?) 화장실에 가도 되나요?

My Favorite Subject Is Music

Words

A Look and write.

| English | math | science | art | music | P.E. | social studies |

1

_____

2

_____

3

_____

4

_____

5

_____

6

_____

7

_____

B Look and match.

1

2

3

4

I like to read maps.

I like to draw pictures.

I like to speak English.

I like to sing songs.

Practice

A Read and write the letter.

What's your favorite subject?

1 My favorite subject is English. ☐

2 My favorite subject is music. ☐

3 My favorite subject is P.E. ☐

4 My favorite subject is art. ☐

ⓐ  ⓑ

ⓒ   ⓓ

B Write and circle.

social studies	science	math	music

1

My favorite subject is _____.

I like to (study math / read books).

2

My favorite subject is _____.

I like to (read maps / draw pictures).

3

My favorite subject is _____.

I like to (play sports / read science books).

4

My favorite subject is _____.

I like to (speak English / sing songs).

Write & Talk

A Write and match.

| I like to speak English. | I like to watch the stars. | I like to draw pictures. |

1

A: My favorite subject is art.

B: _____

ⓐ

2

A: My favorite subject is science.

B: _____

ⓑ

3

A: My favorite subject is English.

B: _____

ⓒ Hello!!

B Read and write.

1 A: What's your favorite subject?

B: My favorite _____ is _____.

2 A: What's your favorite sport?

B: _____ is _____.

3 A: What's your favorite animal?

B: _____ is the _____.

4 A: What's your favorite fruit?

B: _____ is the _____.

| math |
| cat |
| apple |
| soccer |

Reading

A **Read and circle T or F.**

My name is Susan.

My favorite subject is art.

I like to draw animals.

I draw many cats and dogs.

Do you like my pictures?

1   Her favorite subject is art.   (T / F)

2   She likes to draw flowers.   (T / F)

3   She likes to play with animals.   (T / F)

4   She draws many cats and dogs.   (T / F)

My name is Chris.

I like to make animal cookies.

I bake cookies on Saturdays.

The animal cookies are cute.

I like them!

5   He likes to make robots.   (T / F)

6   He bakes cookies on Sundays.   (T / F)

7   The animal cookies are cute.   (T / F)

8   He likes his cookies.   (T / F)

Build Up

A **Complete and write the letter.**

read	study	listen	play	watch	sing

1 I like to _____ songs. ☐

2 Lily likes to _____ to music. ☐

3 She _____ math. ☐

4 I _____ the stars. ☐

5 My brother _____ basketball. ☐

6 Jack _____ science books. ☐

ⓐ  ⓑ  ⓒ

ⓓ  ⓔ  ⓕ

42

A Make the sentence.

1 _____

(your / subject / What's / favorite / ?) 네가 가장 좋아하는 과목은 무엇이니?

2 _____

(favorite / subject / is / My / science / .) 내가 가장 좋아하는 과목은 과학이야.

3 _____

(favorite / What's / your / sport / ?) 네가 가장 좋아하는 운동 경기는 무엇이니?

4 _____

(the lion / favorite / is / My / animal / .) 내가 가장 좋아하는 동물은 사자야.

5 _____

(I / math / to / study / like / .) 나는 수학 공부하는 것을 좋아해.

6 _____

(to / He / likes / draw / pictures / .) 그는 그림 그리는 것을 좋아해.

7 _____

(you / English / to / like / Do / speak / ?) 너는 영어 말하는 것을 좋아하니?

We'll Make Cookies Tomorrow

Words

Ⓐ Look and match.

1 · · have · · to the water park

2 · · meet · · Nick

3 · · pick · · a picnic

4 · · go · · apples

Ⓑ Look and write.

| catch fish | make cookies | plant trees | play games |

1 I'll _____.

2 I'll _____.

3  I'll _____.

4  I'll _____.

Practice

A Read and write the letter.

1 I'll plant trees tomorrow. ☐

2 I'll catch fish tomorrow. ☐

3 I'll make cookies tomorrow. ☐

4 I'll play games tomorrow. ☐

ⓐ  ⓑ

ⓒ  ⓓ

B Look and write.

| meet Nick   have a picnic   go to the water park   pick apples |

1

A: I'll _____ tomorrow.
   Can you join me?
B: Sure.

2

A: I'll _____ tomorrow.
   Can you join me?
B: Sure.

3

A: I'll _____ tomorrow.
   Can you join me?
B: Sure.

4

A: I'll _____ tomorrow.
   Can you join me?
B: Sure.

Write & Talk

A Write and circle.

1

A: I'll _____ tomorrow.
Can you join me?

B: (Sure. / Sorry, I can't.)

make cookies

have a picnic

pick apples

2

A: We'll _____ this weekend.
Can you join us?

B: (Sure. / Sorry, I can't.)

3

A: We'll _____ this Saturday.
Can you join us?

B: (Sure. / Sorry, I can't.)

B Look, choose, and write.

1

A: _____

Can you join me?

B: _____ Sounds fun.

2

A: _____

Can you join us?

B: _____ I'm busy.

ⓐ We'll catch fish this weekend.　　ⓑ We'll play games tomorrow.

ⓒ I'll go to the water park tomorrow.　　ⓓ I'll plant trees this weekend.

46

Reading

Ⓐ Read and write.

Tomorrow is Saturday.

My family will _____ to Uncle's farm.

Uncle _____ many orange trees.

We will _____ oranges and _____ pies.

In the afternoon, we will go to the river.

We will _____ big fish.

We will eat the fish for dinner.

It _____ fun. I can't wait!

| has | pick | go | catch | make | will be |

Ⓑ Look and write.

1 tomorrow
A: I'll _____.
   Can you join _____?
B: Okay.

2 this Sunday
A: I'll _____.
   Can you _____ _____?
B: Sure.

3 this weekend
A: We'll _____.
   _____ _____ join us?
B: Sorry, I can't.

Build Up

(A) Change and write.

1 | I will | — | I'll |

2 | We'll | — | |

3 | He will | — | |

4 | She'll | — | |

5 | We will | — | |

6 | They'll | — | |

(B) Look and write.

| fly a drone | play baseball | bake bread | have a picnic | meet friends |

1

I will _____ tomorrow.

2

He _____ this weekend.

3

We _____ this Sunday.

4

They _____ next weekend.

5

He _____ tomorrow.

Writing

A Make the sentence.

1 _____

(tomorrow / will / cookies / make / I / .) 나는 내일 쿠키를 만들 거야.

2 _____

(He / apples / tomorrow / will / pick / .) 그는 내일 사과를 딸 거야.

3 _____

(will / have / We / this weekend / a picnic / .) 우리는 이번 주말에 소풍을 갈 거야.

4 _____

(trees / She / plant / will / this Sunday / .) 그녀는 이번 일요일에 나무를 심을 거야.

5 _____

(go / will / to the water park / this weekend / I / .) 나는 이번 주말에 워터파크에 갈 거야.

6 _____

(you / me / Can / join / ?) 너는 나와 함께할래?

7 _____

(fun / will / It / be / .) 그것은 재미있을 거야.

What Will You Do This Summer?

Words

Ⓐ Look and write the letter.

ⓐ visit the art museum	ⓑ learn Chinese	ⓒ join a summer camp
ⓓ read many books	ⓔ take swimming lessons	ⓕ go to the beach

1

2

3

4

5

6

Ⓑ Check and write.

1

	visit my grandparents
	meet friends

I'll _____.

2

	have a picnic
	go on a trip

I'll _____.

Practice

Ⓐ Look and match.

1  •

2  •

3  •

4  •

• ⓐ I'll go to the beach.

• ⓑ I'll visit my grandparents.

• ⓒ I'll take swimming lessons.

• ⓓ I'll read many books.

Ⓑ Look and choose.

1

What will you do this summer?
ⓐ I will learn Chinese.
ⓑ I will learn English.

2

What will you do this summer?
ⓐ I will have a picnic.
ⓑ I will go on a trip.

3

What will you do this summer?
ⓐ I will join a summer camp.
ⓑ I will go to the beach.

4

What will you do this summer?
ⓐ I will visit my grandparents.
ⓑ I will visit the art museum.

Write & Talk

A Look and write.

| read many books | learn Chinese | visit my grandparents |

1

weekend

A: What will you do this weekend?

B: I'll _____.

2

winter

A: What will he do _____?

B: He'll _____.

3

summer

A: What will she do _____?

B: She'll _____.

B Read and number in order.

☐ I'll go to the beach.

1 What will you do this weekend?

☐ I'll swim with my friend.

☐ What will you do there?

☐ Sounds great. Have a good time.

5 I'll ride a boat, too.

Reading

A Read and circle T or F.

What will you do this winter, Tiara?

I'll go on a trip to Sydney.

It will be summer there.

I will go to the beach.

I will go to the zoo and meet koalas.

I will join a summer Christmas party, too.

Your friend, Alice

1 Alice will go on a trip this winter.   (T / F)

2 She will go to the museum in Sydney.   (T / F)

3 She will meet friends at the zoo.   (T / F)

4 She will join a Christmas party in Sydney.   (T / F)

B Read, match, and write.

1

A: What will you do this weekend?

B: I will _____.

2

A: What will Mike do this winter?

B: He will _____.

3

A: What will Jessy do this summer?

B: She will _____.

ⓐ this summer

ⓑ this weekend

ⓒ this winter

Build Up

Ⓐ Unscramble and write. Then match.

1

A: What _____ tomorrow?
(do / you / will)

B: _____ visit the art museum.

ⓐ

2

A: What _____ this winter?
(they / will / do)

B: _____ join a winter camp.

ⓑ

3

A: What _____ this weekend?
(Jane / will / do)

B: _____ clean her room.

ⓒ

4

A: What _____?
(will / this summer / do / he)

B: _____ read many books.

ⓓ

5

A: What _____?
(this Sunday / Bob / do / will)

B: _____ go fishing with his dad.

ⓔ

 Writing

Ⓐ Make the sentence.

1 _____

(this summer / What / do / will / you / ?) 너는 이번 여름에 무엇을 할 거니?

2 _____

(do / will / What / this weekend / you / ?) 너는 이번 주말에 무엇을 할 거니?

3 _____

(there / do / will / What / you / ?) 너는 거기서 무엇을 할 거니?

4 _____

(will / I / my / visit / grandparents / .) 나는 내 조부모님을 방문할 거야.

5 _____

(swimming lessons / I / take / will / .) 나는 수영 레슨을 받을 거야.

6 _____

(join / will / She / a summer camp / .) 그녀는 여름 캠프에 참가할 거야.

7 _____

(He / read / will / books / many / .) 그는 많은 책을 읽을 거야.

What Did You Do Yesterday?

Words

A Look and match.

1

2

3

4

helped	badminton
cleaned	my dad
played	my room
listened	to music

B Look and write.

1

I _____.

2

I _____.

visited my aunt

stayed home

played basketball

watched a movie

3

I _____.

4

I _____.

Practice

A Look and choose.

1

What did you do yesterday?

ⓐ I played tennis.　　ⓑ I stayed home.

2

What did you do yesterday?

ⓐ I listened to music.　　ⓑ I watched TV.

3

What did you do yesterday?

ⓐ I visited the museum.　　ⓑ I cleaned my room.

B Read and write the letter.

ⓐ 　　ⓑ 　　ⓒ 　　ⓓ

1
A: What did you do yesterday?
B: I played badminton.

2
A: What did you do yesterday?
B: I watched a movie.

3
A: What did you do yesterday?
B: I helped my dad.

4
A: What did you do yesterday?
B: I visited my aunt.

Write & Talk

A Look and write.

| helped my mom | visited her uncle | cleaned my room | listened to music |

1 A: What did you do yesterday?

B: I _____.

2 A: What did you do yesterday?

B: I _____.

3 A: What did she do yesterday?

B: She _____.

4 A: What did he do yesterday?

B: He _____.

B Read, choose, and write.

A: 1 _____

B: I stayed home all day.

    I washed my dog.

    2 _____

A: I helped my mom.

    3 _____

B: Sounds good.

ⓐ How about you?

ⓑ I baked bread with her.

ⓒ What did you do yesterday?

Reading

A Read and write.

Dan _____ his grandfather yesterday.

He _____ a great time with his grandfather.

They played _____.

They listened to rap music and _____, too.

Rap music is Dan's favorite music.

At night, they _____ the stars together.

"The stars are beautiful."

It was a _____ day for Dan.

| great | visited | computer games | had | watched | danced |

B Read A and circle T or F.

1 Dan stayed home yesterday.   (T / F)

2 Dan played computer games with his uncle.   (T / F)

3 Dan listened to music with his grandfather.   (T / F)

4 Hip-hop music is Dan's favorite music.   (T / F)

5 Dan watched the stars at night.   (T / F)

Build Up

Ⓐ Correct and rewrite.

1 I <u>listen</u> to music yesterday.

    ⋯▸ _____

2 I <u>visit</u> my aunt yesterday.

    ⋯▸ _____

3 She <u>cleans</u> the house yesterday.

    ⋯▸ _____

4 He <u>stays</u> home yesterday.

    ⋯▸ _____

5 They <u>play</u> badminton yesterday.

    ⋯▸ _____

6 The boy <u>washes</u> his dog yesterday.

    ⋯▸ _____

7 They <u>watch</u> a movie yesterday.

    ⋯▸ _____

A Make the sentence.

1
_____

(did / do / you / What / yesterday / ?) 너는 어제 무엇을 했니?

2
_____

(all day / I / home / stayed / .) 나는 하루 종일 집에 있었어.

3
_____

(dad / helped / I / my / .) 나는 아빠를 도왔어.

4
_____

(yesterday / cleaned / She / her room / .) 그녀는 어제 그녀의 방을 청소했어.

5
_____

(uncle / his / He / visited / yesterday / .) 그는 어제 그의 삼촌을 방문했어.

6
_____

(watched / They / together / the stars / .) 그들은 함께 별을 봤어.

7
_____

(his / grandfather / had / He / a great time / with / .)
그는 그의 할아버지와 아주 좋은 시간을 보냈어.

Words

A Look and write.

visited the palace	planted flowers	baked bread
watched a magic show	joined a science camp	practiced the guitar

1

_____

2

_____

3

_____

4

_____

5

_____

6

_____

B Check and write.

1

☐ played at the park

☐ visited my friend

I _____.

2

☐ watched a movie

☐ painted a picture

I _____.

Practice

Ⓐ Look and match.

1

2

3

ⓐ I watched a magic show.

ⓑ I practiced the guitar.

ⓒ I played at the park.

Ⓑ Look and choose.

1

A: How was your weekend?
B: It was good.
  ⓐ I painted a picture.   ⓑ I cleaned my room.

2

A: How was your weekend?
B: It was fun.
  ⓐ I watched TV.   ⓑ I baked bread.

3

A: How was your weekend?
B: It was great.
  ⓐ I stayed home.   ⓑ I visited the palace.

4

A: How was your weekend?
B: It was okay.
  ⓐ I planted flowers.   ⓑ I joined a summer camp.

Write & Talk

A Look and write.

| practiced the guitar | watched a magic show | baked bread |

1

good

A: How was your weekend?

B: It was _____. I _____.

2

great

A: How was your weekend?

B: It _____ _____. I _____.

3

fun

A: I _____ yesterday.

B: How was it?

A: It _____ _____.

B Read, choose, and write.

| ⓐ It was fun. | ⓑ How was school today? |
| ⓒ What did you do? | ⓓ I played at the park. |

1

A: _____

B: It was good.

A: _____

B: I planted trees in the garden.

2

A: How was your weekend?

B: _____

A: What did you do?

B: _____

Reading

Ⓐ Read and write.

It's Jenny TV. I'm your friend, Jenny.

_____ school today?

Was it good?

Here's a message from Roy.

It _____ a fun day.

I _____ a big picture on the wall.

It was for the _____.

I painted the music band.

My friends _____ my picture. Look!

That's great!

liked	painted	was
school concert		How was

Ⓑ Write and choose.

1
A: _____ _____ your weekend?
B: It was good. I planted flowers.

 ⓐ  ⓑ

2
A: _____ did you _____ yesterday?
B: I played at the beach.

 ⓐ  ⓑ

3
A: _____ your weekend?
B: It was fun. I joined a science camp.

 ⓐ  ⓑ

4
A: _____ you do yesterday?
B: I visited the palace.

 ⓐ  ⓑ

Build Up

(A) Write and match.

| was | is | were | are |

1 It _____ cloudy today.

2 I _____ at the park yesterday.

3 He _____ sick yesterday.

4 We _____ at home now.

5 She _____ at the museum yesterday.

6 They _____ angry yesterday.

7 It _____ rainy yesterday.

ⓐ

ⓑ

ⓒ

ⓓ

ⓔ

ⓕ

ⓖ

A Make the sentence.

1 _____

(weekend / How / your / was / ?) 네 주말은 어땠니?

2 _____

(was / How / today / school / ?) 오늘 학교는 어땠니?

3 _____

(did / What / you / yesterday / do / ?) 너는 어제 무엇을 했니?

4 _____

(yesterday / joined / I / a science camp / .) 나는 어제 과학 캠프에 참가했어.

5 _____

(I / watched / yesterday / a magic show / .) 나는 어제 마술 쇼를 봤어.

6 _____

(at / played / We / the park / .) 우리는 공원에서 놀았어.

7 _____

(trees / I / the garden / planted / in / .) 나는 정원에 나무를 심었어.

2nd Edition

LET'S GO

to the English World

4B